BREAKING THE CYCLE

by
Willie Deeanjlo White

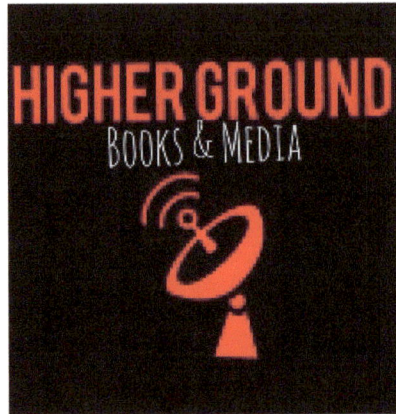

Higher Ground Books & Media
Springfield, Ohio.
http://highergroundbooksandmedia.com

Printed in the United States of America 2019

Dedication

This Book is Dedicated to the My Shero's and Hero's; First and Foremost God's awesome forces of nature that He used to protect, guide, nurture and inspire me, my Grandmothers Mrs. Lillie Mae White, Mrs. Jennitha McWhorter and my Mom the one and only Mrs. Marcella White. They all raised me to feel like one very special young man. In God's awesome plan the Men that chose to be there will never be underrepresented, thank You to my Grandfathers Frank White and David Godfrey who showed me the real meaning of manhood, and lastly without my Father Willie E. White there would have been no Willie D. White.

I would be remiss in not mentioning my Super Hero Siblings who have always been there and together we are indestructible, J. Marcell White, Jeannine R. White and Richard E. White.

Preface

This booklet is intended to enrich all those who it reaches. As in any time we minister to God's people the first person reached by a message is the messenger. As I developed this booklet, it became clear quickly that it is not my actions that needed changing; it is my thought process that determines my attitude. I have always subscribed to the attitude that you have to live your way into a new way of thinking, but the Bible says in Proverbs 23:7, "For as he thinketh in his heart, so is he: …". The key to this verse is thinketh in his heart, sometimes the distance from the head to the heart is an enormous journey. In the process of changing the way the heart functions it is important to apply the correct information. See until now I just assumed that if the behavior change was just positive then it would be enough to change the thinking process and that is true to some degree. What I am learning through applying these concepts to my life is that when the behavior change lines up with the word of God then the change in the thinking not only affects the mind, but it also transforms the heart. When there is true change in the heart it will be even more obvious in the change in behavior, and the cycle should continue to enrich the individual. The more the Word of God penetrates the heart the more the behavior will change, the more the behavior changes the more penetrable the heart becomes. So, to the reader, open your heart and allow God to do the work.

Table of Contents

Opening

Father GOD! I thank You for being Who You are in our lives. I thank You for the life that You so freely have given us this day. I thank You for just being aware of who You are and in the revelation of Who's we are. I ask that you grant the reader of this information Your divine revelation and that Your Word will penetrate their hearts to create the change needed to sustain their growth. I speak health, love peace and joy into their lives and pray for Your continued guidance throughout this process. In Jesus Name A Man!

Chapter One-Learning How

It is important that you understand that it is the way you think that make you do what you do, and if you learn how to think the way God planned for you to think. You will be able to live Gods way, the right way. The Bible tells you to think positive things,

Philippians 4:8 Finally, brethren, whatsoever things are true, whatsoever things are honest, whatsoever things are just, whatsoever things are pure, whatsoever things are lovely, whatsoever things are of good report; if there be any virtue, and if there be any praise, think on these things.

📖(In the spaces provided after each definition, take a few minutes and think about what you read and then make a list of things from your life that match. For example, following the definition of the term True don't just repeat the definition, provide your own personal examples of things you know are True for example; Jesus Loves Me! Or I love summer vacation. The Idea is to develop a list of positive reminders that will help you retrain your brain)📖(This symbol means follow the directions and/you need to write something in the space provided)

Let's look at the suggested thought process

1. *True :(Greek) alhthV alethes al-ay-thace': true (as not concealing):--true, truly, truth.(Strong's)*

a. true: Consistent with fact or reality; not false or erroneous. Truthful.

    1.   Real; genuine. Synonyms authentic.

    2.   Reliable; accurate: *a true prophecy.*

    3.   Faithful, as to a friend, vow, or cause; loyal. Synonyms faithful (Dictionary.com)

📖 _____

_____

_____

_____

_____

2. *Honest: (Greek) semnoV semnos sem-nos': venerable, i.e. honorable:--grave, honest..(Strong's)*

b. honest: Marked by or displaying integrity; upright: *an honest lawyer.*

    1.   Equitable; fair: *honest wages for an honest day's work.*

        a.   Characterized by truth; not false: *honest reporting.*

        b.   Sincere; frank: *an honest critique.*

    2.   Of good repute; respectable.

    3.   Virtuous; chaste. (Dictionary.com)

📖 _____

_____

_____

_____

_____

3 .*Just: (Greek) dikaioV dikaios dik'-ah-yos,(Strong's)*

1. guided by truth, reason, justice, and fairness: We hope to be just in our understanding of such difficult situations.

2. done or made according to principle; equitable; proper: a just reply.

3. based on right; rightful; lawful: a just claim.

4. in keeping with truth or fact; true; correct: a just analysis.

5. given or awarded rightly; deserved, as a sentence, punishment, or reward: a just penalty.

6. in accordance with standards or requirements; proper or right: just proportions.

7. (esp. in Biblical use) righteous.

8. actual, real, or genuine. (Dictionary.com)

📖 _____
_____
_____
_____
_____

4. *Lovely:(Greek) prosjilhV prosphiles pros-fee-lace': friendly towards, i.e. acceptable:-- lovely(Strong's).*

c. lovely: Full of love; loving.

1. Inspiring love or affection.

2. Having beauty that appeals to the emotions as well as to the eye. Synonyms beautiful.

3. Enjoyable; delightful. (Dictionary.com)

📖 _____
_____
_____
_____
_____

5. *Good Report :(Greek): eujhmoV euphemos yoo'-fay-mos: well spoken of, i.e. reputable:--of good report (Strong's)*

d. good: Being positive or desirable in nature; not bad or poor: *a good experience; good news from the hospital.*

a. Having the qualities that are desirable or distinguishing in a particular thing: *a good exterior paint; a good joke.*

b. Serving the desired purpose or end; suitable: *Is this a good dress for the party?*

d. report: An account presented usually in detail.

1. Common talk; rumor or gossip: *According to report, they eloped.*

2. Reputation; repute: *a person of bad report.* (Dictionary.com)

📖 _____
_____
_____
_____
_____

6. *Virtue: :(Greek) areth arete ar-et'-ay: properly, manliness (valor), i.e. excellence (intrinsic or attributed):--praise, virtue (Strong's)*

e. virtue: Moral excellence and righteousness; goodness.

a. An example or kind of moral excellence: *the virtue of patience.* (Dictionary.com)

📖 _____
_____
_____
_____
_____

7. *Praise: :(Greek) epainoV epainos ep'-ahee-nos: laudation; concretely, a commendable thing:--praise (Strong's)*

f. praise: Expression of approval, commendation, or admiration.

1. The extolling or exaltation of a deity, ruler, or hero. (Dictionary.com)

📖 _____
_____
_____
_____
_____

Chapter Two-My Surrounding

Take a minute and ask yourself, do the things that I think about a lot fall into one of these categories? If not, then it is your responsibility to change the way you think. Remember that everything you do starts with the way you think. A part of growing up is learning to develop positive thinking habits. You are a product of your surroundings you will think about the things you do and who you do them with, so get in the habit of being around positive Godly people. If you find yourself getting in trouble a lot for making bad choices, take a moment and look at your friends and the places you hang out.

Ask yourself:

A: Are the people that I am hanging around the kind of people that my parents would like?

B: Do we do the kind of things that we can do in front of my parents?

C: Are we talking about the kinds of things I can talk about in front of my parents?

(Make a list of the things you are doing that you need to change (CONS) and make a list of positive things you like that you need to do more of (PROS)

📖CONS)_____   📖(PROS)_____
_____   _____
_____   _____
_____   _____
_____   _____
_____   _____
_____   _____
_____   _____
_____   _____
_____   _____
_____   _____
_____   _____
_____   _____

Remember the people you hang around, the things y'all do, and most importantly the stuff that you talk about, all change the way **<u>you</u>** talk. The things you talk about make you do the stuff you do.

Chapter Three-My Desires

As we grow up we are tested sometimes to see if we are going to do the right thing, but Christ understands that even though you want to do the right thing, sometimes it is hard to do. In the Bible in Romans it talks about how even if we want to do the right thing, we can't because the sin nature of the human body will not let it. *Romans 7:18 I know that good doesn't live in me-that is, in my body. The desire to do good is inside of me but I can't do it. Romans 7:19 I don't do the good that I want to do, but I do the evil that I don't want to do.(Common English)* But God follows through to tell us that nothing is impossible when you let GOD to do the work. *Matthew 19:26 Jesus looked at them carefully and said, "It's impossible for human beings. But all things are possible for God." (Common English)*

When I think about that part "all things," it makes me ask does God really mean everything?

- Can I resist peer pressure?

- Can I resist anger?

- Can I resist lust?

- Can I resist wanting to do the things that seem like fun, but I know that I am not allowed to do?

- Can I resist me?

(Make a list of the things that you struggle with the most)

📖 _____
_____
_____
_____
_____
_____
_____

Sometimes the hardest stuff to stop doing is the stuff that you do all by yourself. You don't need any help to get into trouble.

Being a young person, you are going to go through the normal process of trying new things. You will look at things that you have never done and wonder what they feel like for example, sex, alcohol, stealing, smoking, running with the rowdy crowd, or even things that seem harmless like staying out all night or driving dad's car when he is asleep. The list of things could go on and on as we all experience growing up in different patterns, what is fun to one will not always excite the other. But the Bible tells us that when we are in Christ, we have the power to do all things. It is the very presence of Christ that gives us the strength *Philippians 4:13 I can do all things through Christ which strengtheneth me.*

Chapter Four-The Battle Ground

What a lot of you <u>who are saved</u> do not know is that the battle that you are going through is not what you think it is. Being children of God we have different battles and even the things that seem like the same battles that our friends are going through for the child of God they are different the bible tells us *Eph 6:12For we wrestle not against flesh and blood, but against principalities, against powers, against the rulers of the darkness of this world, against spiritual wickedness in high places.*

Flesh and blood means other human beings, so we are not at war with each other but against principalities(order of angels that have followed satin),powers(satin delegated influence), the rulers of the darkness (hidden name of satin) (shaded or obscure places) of this world(current consciousness),spiritual(supernatural) wickedness(depravity, sin) in high places(high in rank of satin's army). No matter what kinds of things you are struggling with, satin is involved in some way.

It may feel like the battle is between your body and your mind and for real it is because the bible says that our sprit which affects our mind and our flesh which is our body are at constant war *Galatians 5:17 For the flesh lusteth against the Spirit, and the Spirit against the flesh: and these are contrary the one to the other: so that ye cannot do the things that ye would. Galatians 5:18-24 But if ye be led of the Spirit, ye are not under the law. Now the works of the flesh are manifest, which are these; <u>Adultery</u>, <u>fornication</u>, <u>uncleanness, lasciviousness</u>, <u>Idolatry</u>, <u>witchcraft</u>, <u>hatred</u>, <u>variance</u>, <u>emulations</u>, <u>wrath</u>, <u>strife</u>, <u>seditions</u>, <u>heresies</u>, <u>Envyings</u>, <u>murders</u>, <u>drunkenness</u>, <u>revellings</u>, <u>and such like</u>: of the which I tell you before, as I have also told you in time past, that <u>they which do such things shall not inherit the kingdom of God</u>. But the fruit of the Spirit is love, joy, peace, longsuffering, gentleness, goodness, faith, Meekness, temperance: against such there is no law. And they that are Christ's have crucified the flesh with the affections and lusts.*

Let us examine first the flesh because it is the flesh that we work so hard to overcome.

📖 (In the space provided take a few minutes and write out your personal examples of how you can relate to these activities, if you have not experienced them write out examples from people in your family or people you know, who have done them. Identifying these behaviors in family members will help you identify traps set for you by the devil. Weather you believe it or not you imitate the behaviors of adults around you more then you listen to their spoken lessons) 📖

- *Adultery:(Greek) moicea moicheia moy-khi'-ah: adultery:--adultery:(Strongs) The parties to this crime, according to Jewish law, were a married woman and a man who was not her husband. The Mosaic penalty was that both the guilty parties should be stoned, and it applied as well to the betrothed as to the married woman, provided she were free.(Smith's). conjugal infidelity. An adulterer was a man who had illicit intercourse with a married or a betrothed woman, and such a woman was an adulteress. Intercourse between a married man and an unmarried woman was fornication. (Easton).* Adultery is when a married person male or female has sex with someone other than their wife or husband.

📖 _____
_____
_____
_____

- *Fornication: (Greek) porneuo porn-yoo'-o; to act the harlot, i.e. (literally) indulge unlawful lust (of either sex), harlotry (including adultery and incest); or (figuratively) practice idolatry:--commit (fornication). (Strong's):* Fornication involves a lot. Sex outside of wedlock is fornication, sex with a close family member is fornication, man to man or woman to woman intercourse is fornication, sex with prostitutes is fornication, sex in any shape form or fashion that is not with your wife if you are a male and with your husband if you are a female is considered fornication.

📖 _____
_____
_____
_____
_____

- *Uncleanness: akaqarsia akatharsia ak-ath-ar-see'-ah: impurity (the quality), physically or morally:--uncleanness. (Strong's)* Uncleanness, this one gets a lot of speculation based on a person's personal belief, but the reality is that if a person is behaving in a way that is against the moral code then their actions are considered unclean. More than a social moral code, but the one that God implemented that begins with Thou Shalt Not's found in Exodus 20 through 23. Whenever you are looking for a moral code to follow, it is always smart to start with the Word and when in doubt about your personal actions and how they will be viewed, ask someone. Chances are that if you need to ask someone if the thing you are doing is considered unclean, it probably is.

📖 _____
_____
_____
_____
_____

- *Lasciviousness: (Greek) aselgeia aselgeia as-elg'-i-a (Strong's) (aselgeia, "licentiousness," "wantonness," "unbridled lust," "shamelessness," "outrageousness"): (International Standard Bible Encyclopedia)* Lasciviousness, Unbridled Lust, let's look at a Bridal or the piece that when put into a horse's mouth will guide him and Lust and intense desire or want that often times feels like a need. When you put all of that together you get intense out of control emotions. Well Lasciviousness even takes it a step farther and included as a synonym debauchery or intense involvement with sensual pleasure. So now we can identify the types of emotions and cravings that are out of control, just think of carrying out every one of your sexual fantasies without regard for anyone else only seeking to satisfy self and you have a brief understanding of Lasciviousness.

📖 _____
_____
_____
_____
_____

- *Idolatry: (Greek) eidwlolatreia eidololatreia i-do-lol-at-ri'-ah: image-worship (literally or figuratively):--idolatry.(Strong's): image-worship or divine honour paid to any created object. (Easton)* Idolatry, worshipping an image can look a lot of different ways so let's look at worship: The honor or homage given to God. We worship in many different ways, but prayer is always an important part. Generally, we get something from the worship process a feeling of comfort and safety and this is where the danger of idolatry is so subtle. First of all, there is no other God except our Lord and Savior Jesus, and He is the only deity to be honored in that way. Pure idolatry is when you worship other things as God or a god. Some people worship the moon and stars for example others worship Jesus's mother, oops, and even others worship big bald fat statues. This type of idolatry is easy to distinguish, and other forms are not so easy. Back to that feeling we get from worship, sometimes we find safety and comfort in things like money, education, our parents, our girlfriends and boyfriends; and before you know it we are putting those things before God without being aware. When you pray that your paycheck comes early you have just committed idolatry, when you find more comfort in her or his arms than you find in God then you have just committed idolatry, when you find yourself seeking to spend more time playing the video game and no time seeking the word of God than you have just committed idolatry.

📖 _____
_____
_____

- *Witchcraft: (Greek) jarmakeia pharmakeia far-mak-i'-ah: medication ("pharmacy"), i.e. (by extension) magic (literally or figuratively):--sorcery, witchcraft. (Strong's)* Witchcraft is the things that are customary practiced by a witch or a person believed to have magic powers. Witchcraft is a tool of satin used to open doors in your spirit where demons can enter in and operate. The person displaying these mystical powers is receiving that ability from satin. Fortune telling, tea leaf reading, horoscope, tarot card reading, palm reading, are all popular forms of witchcraft. Witchcraft is not always so obvious it is embedded in our culture and introduced in many subtle ways. The magician at a childhood party is in fact a sorcerer or male witch. The card tricks and magic tricks that are commonly toyed with are a tool used to get you interested in this satanic practice. Many of today's cartoons and video games are devoted to the occult, sorcery and wizardry imagery all open investigative doors in the minds of our young people. Once you are hooked on the delusion of power in order to take it to the next level you will require demonic assistance. Any such activities are all forms of witchcraft and should be avoided. I know the term medication is going to get your attention, but remember Jesus chose a physician, Dr. Luke, as one of his apostle's. This leads me to believe that medication is not evil in and of itself, but the specific use of medication determines its affects. The type of medication that is considered witchcraft is any potion or pill that is developed to overtake a person's will or their ability to make decisions such as a love potion. This is in line with the image of a witch that is displayed in books and movies as a woman over a big pot cooking up some mystical concoction used for various causes and cures. Much like today's medications which are used to cure and treat many physical ailments. Even these medications when improperly administered have a controlling or mind-altering affect and have the ability to overtake a person. For this reason, all forms of medication should be administered under the supervision of a physician. Alcohol, Cocaine, Marijuana and Heroin all have some medicinal purposes, but are so powerful that they are often used by satin for their bewitching powers.

📖 _____

_____
_____
_____
_____
_____

- *Hatred: (Greek) ecqra echthra ekh'-thrah: hostility; by implication, a reason for opposition:-- enmity, hatred.(Strong's)* Hatred is the action form of hate: intense animosity or dislike, to detest. . Hatred is a feeling of antagonism that is so strong that it prompts the person to respond in violence. Hatred is stronger than simple dislike of someone, it is usually birthed out of some sort of resentment were you feel that you were done wrong by the other individual i.e. stolen girlfriend or boyfriend, being molested by a trusted adult, being abandoned by a father or mother, being talked about behind your back by your best friend. The list could go on forever for the reasons why we make it okay to feel such a strong emotion toward others. Hate is a feeling that if left unaddressed will eat away at your spirit causing bitterness and un-forgiveness and will even cause health problems.

📖 _____

_____
_____
_____
_____
_____

- *Variance (Greek) eriV eris er'-is: a quarrel, i.e. (by implication) wrangling:--contention, debate, strife, variance.(Strong's)* Variance the state or fact of differing or being in conflict. This is a need or a feeling of wanting to argue just to argue, this state causes separation in the group.

📖 _____
_____
_____
_____
_____

- *Emulation (Greek) zhloV zelos dzay'-los: properly, heat, i.e. (figuratively) "zeal" (in a favorable sense, ardor; in an unfavorable one, jealousy, as of a husband (figuratively, of God), or an enemy, malice):--emulation, envy(-ing), fervent mind, indignation, jealousy, zeal.(Stong's)* Emulation is not just being jealous of another, but wanting what that person has and setting out on a mission to get it. To Emulate means to imitate the function of, so emulation is doing what someone else does exactly the way you see them do it in hopes of being better at it than they are, but this is not just to be better this is solely to obtain what they have and be better than they are.

📖 _____
_____
_____
_____
_____

- *Wrath (Greek) qumoV thumos thoo-mos': passion (as if breathing hard):--fierceness, indignation, wrath. (Strong's)* Wrath is intense forceful violent anger. It is the form of anger responsible for revenge murder. It is a form of anger that is so intense that it is blinding. Wrath is almost always birthed out of a personal attach of some sort i.e. rape, murder of family member, etc.

📖 _____
_____
_____
_____
_____

- *Strife (Greek) eriqeia eritheia er-ith-i'-ah: properly, intrigue, i.e. (by implication) faction:-- contention (-ious), strife. (Strong's)* Strife is a heated conflict, usually involving physical violence. It consists of an inability to agree accompanied by a conflict or struggle including but not limited to a fight.

📖 _____
_____
_____
_____
_____

- *Seditions (Greek) dicostasia dichostasia dee-khos-tas-ee'-ah: disunion, i.e. (figuratively) dissension:--division, sedition. (Strong's)* Sedition is inciting division with gossip. When you express your negative feelings about the leadership to your peers in the hope of persuading them to feel the same way you do about a particular situation, i.e. Sunday School, Regular School, Parents Rules, etc.

- *Heresies (Greek) airesiV hairesis hah'-ee-res-is: properly, a choice, i.e. (specially) a party or (abstractly) disunion:--heresy (which is the Greek word itself), sect. (Strong's)* Heresies is expressing a personal opinion of a belief or doctrine that is not accepted in the particular setting. For example, if you come to an Apostolic, Pentecostal assembly for the sole purpose of arguing that Jesus is not God. You are not only attempting to incite a riot, but you just might get beat up Ha! Ha!

📖 _____
_____
_____
_____
_____

- *Envying: (Greek) jqonoV phthonos fthon'-os: ill-will (as detraction), i.e. jealousy (spite):-- envy.(Strong's)* Envying is a feeling of discontent or not being satisfied with self that is brought on by comparing yourself to someone else. Envy is desiring the things of others to the point that you cannot feel okay about what you have due to it just not being what they have. You can have all of the things that this other person has, but because of envy you will find things wrong with your stuff just because it is that your stuff.

📖 _____
_____
_____
_____
_____

- *Murders (Greek) jonoV phonos fon'-os: (to slay); murder:--murder, + be slain with, slaughter. (Strong's)* Murder is the unlawful killing of one human by another. There is a special emphasis put of the act if it can be proved to be premeditated or pre planned. The issue attached to murder is the thinking process, in order for you to get into a process of thought that would cause you to take the life of another human being then you would have to leave all morality and enter into a process of thought that is against ever moral code known to man.

📖 _____
_____
_____
_____

- *Drunkenness (Greek) meqh methe meth'-ay: an intoxicant, i.e. (by implication) intoxication:-- drunkenness. (Strong's)* Drunkenness is more than simply being intoxicated on alcohol. The Greek word methe means intoxicant which includes all things that cause you to feel high or intoxicated i.e.

alcohol, marijuana, cocaine, acid, pills, ecstasy, pcp, or another thing that causes you to loose inhibitions or the conscious or unconscious ability to restrain yourself from acting out on a desire or urge . When under the influence, you are more likely to do or say things that you would not normally do or say. Satin will take advantage of the state and initiate the thought for you to open up spiritual doors i.e. sex, homosexuality, thievery or things like that which will lead you down paths that have the ability to destroy you. Under the influence you are less likely to be able to resist his advances and once the door is open it must be closed or will continue to affect you even in your saved life. Drunkenness opens the door for addiction which opens the door for all of the demonic influence that comes with being addicted and living the lifestyle of the addict. In order to continue that process the addict is forced to continually expose him or herself to the places that Satin enjoys and openly functions. Yes, yes, yes the bible says that Jesus was in attendance at a party that served wine and we assume that he drank it as well, but the bible does not say that he actually drank the wine; he created the wine from the water. Now wine was a part of the regular diet and was not looked down upon to consume until it was consumed in excess. But remember that lowering of inhibitions or the ability to say no, takes place well before you are considered drunk, so any consumption of an intoxicating substance has its risks.

📖 _____

_____

_____

_____

_____

- *Revellings (Greek) kwmoV komos ko'-mos: a carousal (as if letting loose):--revelling, rioting. (Strongs)* Revelling is the combination of all of the above, but to the extreme. Cutting loose or rioting are the outward appearance of this process one definition uses the phrase, "To take great pleaser or delight". (Dictionary.com) This leads me to the feeling of complete indulgence in what ever it is that you are doing, especially when that thing is against the will of God for your life. Revelling is more simply put is being completely out of control.

📖 _____

_____

_____

_____

_____

They which do such things shall not inherit the kingdom of God. This is a warning, it is sometimes viewed as a negative thing that God would give an ultimatum, but He doesn't, He gives absolute truths. You can look at it anyway you want too but the reality is God is God and who are we to question His Wisdom. The bible tells us that His thoughts are not able to be understood by the human understanding or intellect. *Isaiah 55:8 For my thoughts are not your thoughts, neither are your ways my ways, saith the LORD. 55:9 For as the heavens are higher than the earth, so are my ways higher than your ways, and my thoughts than your thoughts.*

God informs you that if these types of behaviors are continued, they produce separation. As young people this is a hard concept to understand, you are in the mindset that needs everything explained. So, he has set up several avenues for you to receive the wisdom and guidance that will help you not have to travel this downward path.

The first and the most important tool used by God is your parents, unfortunately this is one of the biggest conflicts between you and your parents. A parent's job is to teach, guide and protect, God instructions in Proverbs, *"Pr 22:6 Train up a child in the way he should go: and when he is old, he will not depart from it"*. Every lesson given to a child by a parent is intended to complete this process.

Does this mean that every decision made by a parent is fair? Absolutely not! Somewhere along the way this concept of fairness has corrupted the minds of our youth. Was it fair for your Mother to have to face death to give you life, Is it fair that your Father is held responsible for your actions no matter what you do, Was it fair that God had to become Man to save His own creation, Was it fair that He would be tortured for crimes He did not commit, Was it fair that He would have to endure death that you might have life, the answer to all these questions is NO. Who told you that life was fair, think about all of the things that you have done that you have not gotten caught for, is that fair? It is funny that the only time we holler about fair, is when we really mean I want it my way. (I will not ask you to write down all of the things you have gotten away with, but I do want you to take a minute and reflect on them.)

Well the bible also teaches us in Proverbs, *"Pr 22:15 Foolishness is bound in the heart of a child; but the rod of correction shall drive it far from him."* Does this mean that parents should physically abuse their children? No! But not to provide appropriate punishment is also warned against,

"Pr 23:13 Withhold not correction from the child: for if thou beatest him with the rod, he shall not die. Proverbs 23:14 Thou shalt

beat him with the rod, and shalt deliver his soul from hell. Pr 29:15 The rod and reproof give wisdom: but a child left to himself bringeth his mother to shame. Pr 29:17 Correct thy son, and he shall give thee rest; yea, he shall give delight unto thy soul. " Withhold not correction is ordained of God as a responsibility for parents. They are required to provide discipline.

I know that you don't believe that this is again fair, but your understanding is limited to your lifetime. Your parents have lived longer and thus seen and experienced more. I know that things are different now than when your parents grew up, but the bible tells us, *"Ec 1:9The thing that hath been, it is that which shall be; and that which is done is that which shall be done: and <u>there is no new thing under the sun</u>. "* It might look new to you because guess what? It is new to you.

My son taught me one of the biggest lessons of my life, I took him to the bank to cash his first pay check and because he seemed mature and I knew he had experience handling money because he spends mine so well, I sent him in and he stood there looking bewildered. I became agitated because as usual I was rushing for time. He then said, "What would make you think that I know how to do this?" You see in my mind this process is second nature, but to him until this point money came from me. This is exactly what happens in a lot of cases, you as young people assume that your opinion of a situation is the only opinion. But as you are now aware there is a <u>war</u> going on in your mind that is attempting to shape that opinion. Satan wants you to be separate from God and any time he can cause separation from your parents then he is one step closer to separating you from God.

Chapter Six-The Strategy and Armor

There is Hope!!! By getting an understanding of the works of the flesh or the way sin operates in our lives, we are better able to identify dangerous activities that will lead us into dangerous territories. Remember we are at war with ourselves and in battle it is always important to study your opponent. To study your opponent in this case you have to begin by taking a look at your past. Think of the times that you allowed these behaviors to function in your life and ask yourself what was going on with me that I allowed it. By doing this you will be making yourself aware of the areas of your life that Satan has the most effect on.

For example, I know that whenever I get around Suzie that my mind always begins to undress her, or when I am around coo Joe my words tend to be more offensive. Then it is safe to say that it is not Suzie or Joe that are the problem, but the affect that Satan has on me when I am around Suzie or Joe. So, what do you want me to do? Avoid all people for the rest of my life that cause my flesh to respond? That would be all most all of my friends.

Did you just think that? Well that is a normal response, Fear! No, I am not saying run from nothing or no one. The key is in building your relationship with God. When you develop that relationship then you will be stronger to resist the influence of satin. Does that mean that you will never be turned on by a member of the opposite sex, No.? But what it does mean is that you will be able to express that attraction in a manner that will not negatively affect your spirit.

When we are led of the Spirit, we will produce certain fruits. There are many types of walks with God, but a fruitless one is a difficult one. As you get closer to Christ, you will begin to notice that you don't respond the way you used too and then and only then will you truly understand the fruits of the spirit.

So we will take a look and them now!

Galatians 5:22-23 But the fruit of the Spirit is love, joy, peace, longsuffering, gentleness, goodness, faith, Meekness, temperance: against such there is no law.

📖(Following each description below take a few minutes and write out at least five examples of how God has shown Himself to you in these areas) 📖

- *Love: agaph agape ag-ah'-pay (Greek); love, i.e. affection or benevolence;(Strong's)* Love is the ability to show comfort, the ability to embrace, the ability to understand, the ability to feel what another person is feeling. Love does not judge, it is willing to go the extra mile, it is also willing to tell the truth. The kind of Love that God has shown to us is more than a feeling it is an action. No one cares what you know until they see how much you care. It is difficult to describe love because it is more than a word it is a way of life.

📖_____

_____

_____

_____

_____

- *Joy: cara chara khar-ah' (Greek); cheerfulness, i.e. calm delight:--gladness, X greatly (Strong's)*
  Joy is more than an outward expression of excitement it is an inner transformation of the spirit. This type of joy is not something that is a result of anything exterior and cannot be taken away. Joy is knowing that no matter what everything is already alright, it is not having to feel worry because it is replaced by faith. Joy is that inner warmth that says I am okay. When joy is on the inside then it makes everything a little easier on the outside.

📖 _____

_____

_____

_____

_____

_____

_____

- *Peace (Greek) eirhnh eirene i-ray'-nay; by implication, prosperity:--one, peace, quietness, rest, + set at one again (Strong's)* Peace is more than mere absence of stress, the peace of the Lord is almost unexplainable. It is like knowing that you know that everything is going to be ok. It is like despite what the situation looks like feeling safe and confident of a positive outcome to that situation and being able to rest before the situation is resolved. The bible says the peace of the Lord is not something the world can give or take away, it is supernatural.

📖 _____

_____

_____

_____

_____

_____

_____

- *Longsuffering (Greek) makroqumia makrothumia mak-roth-oo-mee'-ah ; ith long (enduring) temper(Strong's).* Longsuffering is being able to put up with a difficult person, event or situation despite personal objection. Longsuffering is not self-sacrifice, it is not staying in an abusive relationship, it is not continuing to be abused by your parents, just because they are your parents, it is not swallowing your opinion just to get along with the crowd. It is however being able to stand strong in difficult situations like being obedient to the voice of God in your life and operating against your normal values. Sometimes God will have you minister to someone you dislike, or He will tell you to stay involved with a school activity that makes you uncomfortable so that your light will shine. Longsuffering is being able to endure these and other uncomfortable situations in a manner that displays the love of God and not your normal begrudging personality. Yes you will be aware of the discomfort, but not be negatively affected by it.

📖 _____

_____
_____
_____
_____
_____
_____

- *Gentleness (Greek) crhstothV chrestotes khray-stot'-ace; morally, excellence (in character or demeanor) (Strong's)* Gentleness is a character trait produced by walking with God. In all that you do, you display the patience and mannerisms of moral excellence. It is more than simply speaking soft or displaying a humble demeanor or outward appearance, it is an internal genuine transformation of character that is evidenced in your outward behavior. This looks like being willing to help, show love and support to friends, being fun to be around because you are just and all-around likeable person.

📖 _____

_____
_____
_____
_____
_____
_____
_____

- *Goodness (Greek) agaqwsunh agathosune ag-ath-o-soo'-nay; virtue or beneficence (Strong's)* Goodness is a quality of the heart. Goodness looks a lot like honesty, integrity, genuineness, wholesomeness. For those of you with that loving caring warm Grandmother you have a good reference for this quality and for those who cannot relate to that example think of how you wanted your Grandma to be. Don't be misled into believing that you have to be an old Grandma to be able to develop this fruit, I just used that as an example for you to have a visualization. Goodness is that character in you that wants to do the right thing; it is that inner voice that always has the positive answer for the negative situation. It just needs to be developed into a character from being a feeling or voice, and only God and your willingness to change can accomplish that development.

📖 _____

_____
_____
_____
_____
_____
_____

- *Faith (Greek) pistiV pistis pis'-tis; persuasion, i.e. credence; moral conviction (of religious truth, or the truthfulness of God or a religious teacher), especially reliance upon Christ for salvation (Strong's).* Faith as a fruit is a way of life. Faith biblically is the substance of things hoped for and the evidence of things not seen, or the physical manifestation of things that you have hoped, dreamed, asked or even wished for and the tangible or touchable and even emotional or spiritual proof of the of things that you have not actually witnessed with your human sense, i.e. touch, taste, smell and sight. Faith believes beyond proof. It is being able to not only act as if something has happened waiting for it to come to pass, but also knowing that despite what your human senses are telling you because of what it looks like that God is able to do that what He told you he would. Being able to stand not only on the Fact that Jesus is the one and only Living God, but also in all of those things in His Word. Faith is a conversion and the actual vehicle by which God moves in our lives. The Bible says without Faith it is impossible to please God. All throughout the Bible God gives us examples that when people were able to have the faith that He could then He would, but for those who doubted Him he was not able to help them. So, in essence your degree or amount of Faith determines God's effectiveness in your life. The way to increase in faith is to first have Faith that He is and then it will grow as you continue to walk with God. Try Him first! There are some things in His word that you must do to tie Him to His promises, You must be born again, You must be Baptized in the Name or Jesus for the remission of sin, You must pay tithe, You must adhere to the things of His word that you are aware of in other words you can't just live any old kind of way and expect God to bless you. He can't bless the mess, he can clean the mess and bless the messer, but you have to first have the faith, get it!!!! And it grows!!!!

Meekness (Greek) praothV praotes prah-ot'-ace; gentleness, by implication, humility. (Strong's) Meekness is a mannerism or way of response. Not being easily provoked by others to respond in a negative manner. It is not simply being humble or soft spoken but being able to carry yourself in a self-assured manner that is not intimidated by the haughtiness or arrogance of others but not being boastful or prideful at the same time. Knowing who you are and allowing others the freedom of expression of who they are. Where God is in this equation is that this fruit allows you to co-exist and prosper in the face of controversy or negative competition.

📖 _____

_____
_____
_____
_____
_____
_____
_____

- *Temperance (Greek) egkrateia egkrateia eng-krat'-i-ah; self-control (Strong's)* Temperance is being aware of yourself at all times and exhibiting the ability to display the appropriate response in all situations. I heard a person preach who said that they want to be so filled with the Holy Ghost that He becomes like their reflex or immediate unconscious response. That to me is the ultimate form of temperance, being able to respond from the spirit and not the flesh. Even when the flesh is screaming to do something different. When your flesh is saying cuss him out, temperance says pray for him and walk away, when your flesh says yeah you are right, they lied to you, temperance says in all things give God the glory. When your flesh says knock him upside the head, temperance says Jesus was patient with you be calm in your response.

📖 _____

_____
_____
_____
_____
_____
_____

Chapter Seven-Your Victory

God says against these there is no law which means they are good. The law was created to bring to the light the fact that people were acting against the Will and Nature of God. The Law revealed sin. Man was already participating in these behaviors because of their inherited desire to do wrong. *Psalms 51:5 Behold, I was shapen in iniquity; and in sin did my mother conceive me.* Coming out of the gate we are drawn to do wrong. You have to teach a child how to do the right thing, not in doing the wrong thing.

Remember these: don't touch the stove it's hot, don't stick things in the socket you will get hurt, get out of that tree or you will fall, you are too young to stay up that late you will regret it in the morning. Don't hang around those kinds of boys or girls you will get into trouble, don't have sex until you are married, and stay in school. Remember that some things are outside of your ability to understand, you really don't know everything. But by guarding your thought process with the proper things of God, then you increase your chances of producing the kind of fruit that please God. So let's revisit His command! Think on these Things.

📖 *(In the space provided write out things that you can use under each category to bring your thoughts back in order when you are having a hard time focusing. They don't have to be the same things that you wrote before.)* 📖

whatsoever things are **true,**

📖 _____

_____

_____

_____

whatsoever things are **honest,**

📖 _____

_____

_____

_____

whatsoever things are **just,**

📖 _____

_____

_____

_____

whatsoever things are **pure,**

📖 _____

_____

_____

_____

whatsoever things are **lovely,**

📖 _____

_____

_____

_____

whatsoever things are **of good report**;

📖 _____

_____

_____

_____

if there be any **virtue,**

📖 _____

_____

_____

_____

and if there be any **praise,**

📖 _____

_____

_____

_____

Ok then what do I do? Is that what you were thinking? Well great!!!!! Jesus is the way. *John 14:6 Jesus saith unto him, I am the way, the truth, and the life: no man cometh unto the Father, but by me.* If you have not accepted Christ as your personal savior than the time is now. *Romans 10:9 That if thou shalt confess with thy mouth the Lord Jesus, and shalt believe in thine heart that God hath raised him from the dead, thou shalt be saved.* It can't be that easy you say! Well of course it is!!!! Just say this short but effective prayer!

SAY IT OUT LOUD!!

Father God forgive me! Forgive me of all sin, sins of commission and sins of omission. I believe in Your Life, I believe in Your Death and I believe in Your Resurrection. Satin I renounce you; you are no longer my god. Jesus come into me. Take my life and lead me in all that I do. I surrender all to you this day as my Lord and Savior. In the mighty name of Jesus I pray.

Amen.

Yes, that is it you have now taken on the name of Christ! Do I need to be baptized? Absolutely! Go to the nearest church and inform them of your resent admission and they will follow through with the water baptism in the name of Jesus. If they are not willing to use the name of Jesus in your baptism then go to the next church or call Greater Grace Temple at (937) 328-3308 in Springfield, Ohio and someone will lead you in the right direction. Is the name of Jesus that important? Absolutely!! *Acts 2:38 Then Peter said unto them, Repent, and be baptized every one of you <u>in the name of Jesus Christ</u> for the remission of sins, and ye shall receive the gift of the Holy Ghost.*

For those of you that have already accepted Christ and been baptized in the name of Jesus I hope that you have grown from this workbook and leave you with this. <u>Say this payer Out Loud!</u>

Father God I surrender all to you this day, I recommit myself to you and ask for your continued care, correction and guidance, Open my eyes to your plan for my life. Take me into the next generation of Your blessing. I ask that you cover me with your protective angels, shielding me from all fiery darts of the adversary and revealing Your perfect will for my life. Bless those that bless me and curse those that curse me. In the mighty name of Jesus I pray Amen!

Remember to always reflect on this workbook to track progress in this area.

Reference:

Easton, M.G.(1897)., Illustrated Bible Dictionary, Thomas Nelson.

Orr, J. (1976). *The International standard Bible encyclopedia / James Orr, general editor.* Grand Rapids: Wm. B. Eerdmans Pub. Co.

Smith, W.G.(2005). *Smith's Bible dictionary / William Smith.* Peabody, MA: Hendrickson Publishers.

Strongs, J. (2007). *Strong's exhaustive concordance of the Bible / James Strong.* Peabody, MA: Hendrickson Publishers.

King James, New King James, American Standard English and World English Bible were all translations of Biblical references in the text.

Other titles from Higher Ground Books & Media:

Wise Up to Rise Up by Rebecca Benston

A Path to Shalom by Steen Burke

Overcomer by Forrest Henslee

Miracles: I Love Them by Forest Godin

32 Days with Christ's Passion by Mark Etter

Knowing Affliction and Doing Recovery by John Baldasare

Out of Darkness by Stephen Bowman

The Magic Egg by Linda Phillipson

The Tin Can Gang by Chuck David

Whobert the Owl by Mya C. Benston

Add these titles to your collection today!

http://highergroundbooksandmedia.com